Harwich and Dovercourt:
the photographs of Alfred Smith

Selected by
David Kindred & Peter Goodwin

Old Pond
PUBLISHING LTD

First published 2010

ISBN 978-1-906853-49-5

A catalogue record for this book is available from the British Library

Published by
Old Pond Publishing Ltd
Dencora Business Centre
36 White House Road
Ipswich
IP1 5LT
United Kingdom

www.oldpond.com

Title page photograph: Harwich and Parkeston, the winners of the Harwich Charity Cup in May 1973.
They beat Clapton 3–0, with goals from Steve Devaux, Dave Allaway and Mal Crissell.
Pictured with the cup are Don James, Dave Allaway, Mick Clarke (hidden) Gordon Pickess,
Steve Page, Tony Armstrong, John French, Reg Smith, Malcolm Crissell and Steve Devaux.

Frontispiece: In April 1976 the Prinz Hamlet was the last of the Prinz line to sail from Harwich.

Cover and book design by Liz Whatling
Printed in Malta by Gutenberg Press

Contents

Page

Introduction 5

Sea and Rail: Harwich and Parkeston Quay 7

Around Harwich and Dovercourt 54

People and Events 83

Sports 116

Acknowledgements 128

Introduction

When freelance commercial photographer Alfred Smith worked in the 1950s-'80s he recorded a historic town that had undergone fundamental changes beginning in the Victorian era and continuing after the Second World War.

Harwich stands on a narrow peninsula in north-east Essex, at the mouths of the Rivers Stour and Orwell. The town has been of great importance since the Middle Ages as it was the only safe haven between the Humber and the Thames.

Harwich was granted borough status in 1318 and the long, proud traditions were confirmed with the King James I Charter of 1604 which continued earlier privileges which had established fairs and markets. This charter created a form of government which survived for centuries in which a Mayor, Aldermen and Councillors appointed by the King were bequeathed with legal and administrative powers. Harwich had two Members of Parliament and is one of only twenty-four boroughs in the country that has the post of High Steward, a position dating back to the 12th century.

Harwich Town Council meets in the Guildhall, which from 1673 to 1953 was used for meetings of the Harwich Borough Council before they moved to the old Great Eastern Hotel on the quay. After the coming of the district council, the town council moved back to the Guildhall. Throughout many years Harwich has been an important port for commercial, passenger, fishing and naval vessels and is the home to Trinity House which controls all the navigational aids around the UK. With its sister port of Parkeston, it is the east coast's 'Gateway to Europe' with ferries crossing the North Sea to ports in Europe.

The town itself was built on a grid system so that the three main streets lay north to south, providing shelter in the narrow streets and alleyways from the easterly winds so prevalent on this part of the east coast.

The old naval shipyard built many a fine vessel for the Navy and trading ships during the period from 1660 to 1827. The town produced many hardy seamen who manned warships, merchantmen and crews for exploration. Among the explorers was Capt. Christopher Newport,

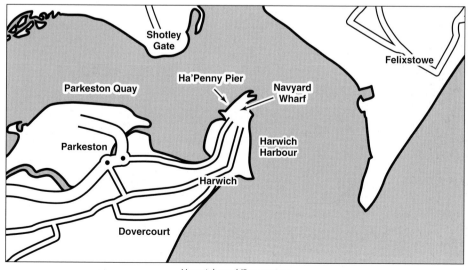

Harwich and Dovercourt

born in Harwich in 1561, who led the expedition to the New World which founded Jamestown in 1607. The master of the *Mayflower*, Christopher Jones, lived in the town. One ill-fated expedition to find the North-West Passage led by Sir John Franklin also sailed from Harwich in the early 1800s.

The maritime history of the town led in 2006 to the building of a memorial sited on the Quay dedicated to seamen lost in peace and war. The memorial was built by the Harwich branch of the Merchant Navy Association.

After the Second World War many town buildings which had fallen into disrepair were demolished as unfit for habitation. This demolition which continued into the 1960s meant that many fine buildings were replaced by sixties-style housing. With hindsight, it might have been better to have restored them to their original style – as a number have recently been done by private individuals.

Whereas Upper Dovercourt dates back to the Domesday Book with All Saints Church founded in the 11th century, the town of Dovercourt is a far more

recent development. Dovercourt's growth began in Victorian times on fields between Upper Dovercourt and Harwich. As more housing was built, it eventually became the main shopping area. Harwich itself suffered, with many of its shops in closing.

The coming of the railways in 1854 led in the 1880s to the building on reclaimed land of Parkeston Quay – now known as Harwich International Port – and the village of Parkeston for the workers. Great Eastern Railway built the new quay when the old quay at Harwich proved to have inadequate space for their North Sea Ferries. Over the years ferries have sailed to all European ports, with modern-day cruise ships now a regular sight.

With the advent of the new quay and station with its own hotel came special 'Boat Trains' to accommodate passengers bound for London and the rest of the UK. Their names became folklore – the 'Hook Continental', 'Day Continental', 'Flushing Continental' and the 'Scandinavian'. At the same time, the 'North Continental' was able to head north via the spur at Manningtree.

Believed to be Parkeston Quay – dock workers with horses which were used in the goods yard for towing wagons.

SEA and RAIL:
Harwich and Parkeston Quay

A Light Vessel similar to LV90, but lacking its lattice tower. LV90 went down on Goodwin Sands on 26 November 1954. In this photograph, probably taken after 1954, the Light Vessel is laying alongside the Trinity House vessel *Ready* which was in service 1947-77 and looks fairly aged here.

Trinity House vessel *Patricia* coming alongside Trinity Pier in the 1950s.

Trinity House vessel *Triton*, the last of the coal-burning Trinity House tenders, alongside Trinity Pier.
Triton was converted to a trawler in 1963.

A former fishing drifter, *Cossa Water*, of Lerwick, being used as a diving tender. The diving platform is alongside and a crowd of interested watchers are seated on the pier, c. 1950s.

The drifter working alongside the pier, probably undertaking work before the new pier was built, c. 1950s.

Gas House Creek in 1960, with numerous craft in the creek, including fishing boat HH65 and *My Summity*, a coaster owned by FT Everard & Sons of Greenhithe.

The crew of a lightship prior to returning to their Light Vessel after leave, c. 1960s.

The harbour in October 1970 from the Train Ferry Terminal. The pilot ship number 19 with a cutter is alongside Trinity Pier. In the background are the Trinity House buoy yard building, the old Great Eastern Railway Hotel, Ha'Penny Pier and Navyard with a Prinz Line vessel alongside.

Navigational buoys being repainted in the buoy shed, c. 1960s.

August 1967 witnessed the arrival of the new lifeboat ON44-005, *Margaret Graham*, officially named on 27 September by Capt. GE Barnard, Deputy Master of Trinity House.

Margaret Graham alongside with her crew in September 1967.

An injured Goanese seaman suffering from head injuries being landed at Ha'Penny Pier on 25 September 1970. The seaman, from the MV *City of Winchester*, was injured in a fall down into the hold. The photograph includes crew members Bob Ramplin, Doctor Corbett, Cox'n Peter Burwood, Aubrey Seaman, Les Smith, Terry Bennett, Ken Brand and a member of the public, Richard 'Pansy' Potter.

On 26 January 1963 Walton & Frinton Lifeboat *Edian Courtald* was on an engine test run after the ice had dispersed at Walton. They went into Harwich to pick up a boat belonging to their coxswain that had broken away from its moorings and had been picked up by THV *Patricia* outside the Cork. Crew, bow to stern: Gilbert Barrs - mechanic, Ken Haggis, Dennis Finch in oilskin - bowman, Jonas Oxley - coxswain, Frank Bloom - 2nd cox, Ron Wyatt and Bobby Kemp.

On 25 January 1963 ex Shoreham Lifeboat ON758 – on passage north as relief lifeboat, believed to be to Whitby – reported they were stuck in the ice in Harwich Harbour. A larger vessel made a passage for ON758 to the open sea. In the background alongside Ha'Penny Pier are *River Lady II* and the dredger, *Landguard*.

Trinity House Pilot Cutter *Valour* in Harwich Harbour, August 1985.

The fishing boat *Why Worry* with Vic Good loading a haul of sprats into baskets. c. 1960s.

A haul of shrimps being sorted. Vic Good and Frankie Pells are aboard the *Girl Elsie*, probably in the 1960s.

Fishing boats HH21 *Girl Elsie* and HH100 *Sweet Waters* alongside in February 1969.

A seaplane of Aquila Airways in the harbour in the mid 1950s.
This was the last commercial seaplane flight out of Harwich.

When the tail rotor spun off, this Westland Whirlwind Air Sea Rescue helicopter from Felixstowe
crashed off Harwich Beach in the early 1960s. It is believed all the crew were killed.
The helicopter is aboard the Trinity House vessel which picked it up.

Fire engine in 1964 on Trinity Pier alongside a Pilot vessel.

Firemen lifting a light portable pump aboard the Pilot vessel to extinguish a fire in the engine room. Station Officer Bill Buckland is appearing from inside the ship; Don Martin is one of the firemen.

A new Pilot Cutter number 32 being lifted into the water in January 1976. The ship alongside is *Rhodri Mawr*.

Minesweeper HMS *Wasperton* on fishery duties with two fishing vessels it had arrested in June 1968.
One is the *Galopin* of Boulogne.

MV *Epping* coming alongside in the 1950s, one of three passenger ferries, along with the *Brightlingsea* and *Hainault* in use in the harbour between Harwich, Shotley and Felixstowe. Built in Portsmouth in 1914 for the LNER, she was requisitioned by the Admiralty during the war and sold by British Railways in 1962.

21

The MV *Brightlingsea* and *Landguard* in the 1960s alongside Ha'Penny Pier, with a lightship
and Shotley in the background.

A 1960s aerial view of Ha'Penny Pier with the BR dredger *Landguard* alongside with two fishing boats in the pound.
One is HH21.

The Conservative Prime Minister Ted Heath and crew striding across the quayside from the Pier Hotel in May 1970.

Ted Heath's yacht *Morning Cloud* which he had bought in 1969, alongside another vessel in the pound.

Round-the-world yachtsman Sir Alec Rose visited the Harwich Lifeboat in May 1969. Left to right: Jeff Sallows, Alec Rose, Derek Gibson (Hon Sec) Peter Burwood, Don Mudd, Les Smith and Terry Bennett.

Light Ship alongside with Trinity House vessel *Patricia* preparing to berth during the 1960s.

Crowds of people on Ha'Penny Pier and along the quay in 1964. *Landguard* and the Trinity House ship *Vestal* are alongside.

Aerial view of Navyard Wharf in 1964 with a vast number of tractors waiting to be loaded aboard the cargo vessel *Traviata* for export.

The Ro-Ro berth in full operation at Navyard in September 1985.

Caravans waiting to be loaded onto the *Aniara*, one of the first bow loaders to use the
Navyard Wharf during the late 1970s.

Blenheim of London departs Parkeston Quay in May 1971.

Prins Hamlet alongside Parkeston Quay in the 1970s.

The construction of Navyard Wharf in 1962, previously a slipway as part of the old ship yard.

Rail wagons being loaded on to the train ferry in 1956.

Cars being loaded onto a train ferry by crane in late 1965.

A car transporter with Minis for export shipment in 1965.

800 HP Paxman diesel D8220 with car transporter from Didcot for shipment aboard the train ferry in 1965.

A shipment of combine harvesters being exported or imported by the train ferry in 1965.

Class 37 6743 diesel locomotive at Harwich Town station March 1970 with a London train. 6743 was withdrawn in January 2000 and scrapped at Sims Metals, Beeston in March 2003.

Train ferry crew, including Mal Bird, Sid Jordan, Rocky Hambling, Paul Gochin and Alex MacLaughlin, enjoying a 'safe arrival' beer and song in March 1977.

Ship's engineer in the train ferry engine room March 1971.

69703 shunting trucks aboard the train ferry in 1956.

The *Norfolk* ferry departs the terminal in March 1970.

J15 locomotive 68617 shunting wagons on to the train ferry in November 1955.

J15 number 65458, fitted with Westinghouse brake and vacuum pipes for use on the
branch passenger service, is running into Dovercourt Bay station.

Tugs *Sauria* and *Cervia* alongside Navyard wharf in December 1968.

The 1960s – a young lad who fell into the water from the quayside is being pulled to safety.

The youngster
being cared for
by his rescuers.

Driver Mr Francis prepares to climb into the cab of Brush diesel (ex1149), c. 1962.

Britannia class Pacific number 70034 'Thomas Hardy' built in 1952 at Crewe, in need of a clean at Parkeston. One of the 'Brits' used to haul the 'Hook Continental', this locomotive was disposed of and cut up in September 1957.

A well-worn Thompson B1, not fitted with electrics or displaying a number.
At Parkeston with the East Signal Box in the background, c. early 1960s.

Hunslet 204 HP D2554 with gate gear change coupled up to a freight train on Parkeston Quay with the
Avalon in the background in 1960.

The *Duke of York*, May 1953. She was en route to Parkeston Quay with 470 passengers and crew in thick fog when she collided with the American ship *Haiti Victory*. The *Duke of York* had her bow section cut off, crew and passengers being taken aboard the *Haiti Victory*, *Norfolk Ferry* and *Dewsbury*. Sadly eight lives were lost. The tug *Empire Race* towed the stricken vessel into Parkeston; she was repaired at Jarrow and returned to service in 1954.

The DFDS vessel *Kronprins Frederick* at Parkeston in May 1954. A year later she caught fire at Parkeston and the entire interior of the ship was destroyed. After refit in Denmark, she re-entered service. Alongside is the *Dewsbury*.

The Dutch North Sea Ferries *Prinses Beatrix* and *Koningin Wilhelmina* at Parkeston in the 1960s.

British Rail ferry
Amsterdam alongside
Parkeston Quay.
Launched in 1950, she
saw service with
BR until 1968.

MV *Stella Polaris* at Parkeston, c. 1952. This elegant vessel was launched in September 1926. Joining the Bergen Line as a luxury cruise ship, she sailed out of New York on world cruises finishing at Harwich. Seized by the Germans during the war, she was used as a recreation centre for U-Boat officers, Handed back to the owners after the war, she underwent an extensive refit and was sold in 1951 to the Clipper line. She continued cruising until 1969 when she was sold to a Japanese company as a floating hotel; she remains in Japan as a tourist attraction.

Rota at Parkeston. She was built in 1923 for DFDS, requisitioned during the war by the British, returned to DFDS in 1945 and scrapped in 1962.

The *Sea Freightliner II* at Parkeston in April 1976, a container ship which plied the North Sea between Harwich and Holland.

Sheringham at Parkeston. Built at Hull for LNER, she was launched and entered service in 1929 on the Harwich–Hoek van Holland route. During the war she was requisitioned by the Royal Navy as a troop ship, then finally scrapped in 1960 in Belgium.

Speedlink Vanguard at Parkeston after collision with the Townsend Thoresen ferry *European Gateway* outbound from Felixstowe to Zeebrugge on Sunday, 19 December 1982. The *European Gateway* capsized onto a sand bank and six on board lost their lives.

A Morris 1000 Traveller being craned aboard the *Koningin Emma* at Parkeston in 1960.

Passengers boarding a Dutch passenger vessel at Parkeston in 1960.

Freight waiting to be craned on board at Parkeston in 1960.

March 1972. The new passenger terminal being constructed at Parkeston, which eliminated the walk along the quayside.

Freight being unloaded at Parkeston in the 1960s.

Mail being hoisted on to the waiting ship, c. 1960s.

Soldiers on guard duty at the Transit Camp being inspected in 1956. The camp was used for the Movement Control of troops to BAOR Germany after the war, many of whom were National Service recruits.

Troops waiting to board a troop ship at Parkeston, probably the *Vienna*, one of three troop ships, the others being *Empire Parkeston* and *Empire Wansbeck*, c. 1950s.

Soldiers from a Scottish regiment waiting to board the troop ship, c. 1950s.

Officers in deep discussion alongside the troop ship *Vienna* in 1956.

Celebratory British Transport police line up at Parkeston, c. 1960s. *Amsterdam* is in the background.

A lucky soul being rescued after being trapped on the ice at Bathside Bay during the winter of 1955 when the sea froze over.

In March 1964 Radio Caroline started broadcasting from the MV *Caroline* moored close to the Cork lightship off Felixstowe. The ship was tendered from Harwich. In May a second ship, the *Mi Amigo*, arrived and moored off Frinton-on-Sea transmitting the programmes of Radio Atlanta. The two stations soon merged with the MV *Caroline* sailing to near the Isle of Man and transmitting as Radio Caroline North. The *Mi Amigo* (pictured) remained off Frinton as the home of Radio Caroline South. The *Mi Amigo* was soon joined by other 'pirate' radio ships. Harwich harbour was the base for tendering until the radio stations were outlawed in August 1967. Radio Caroline broadcast from the *Mi Amigo* for many more years until she sank in a storm in 1980.

The broadcast studio on the *Mi Amigo* in 1965 with station founder
Ronan O'Rahilly (left) and engineer Patrick Starling at the controls.

The crew on board the *Mi Amigo* in 1965.

A radio engineer with the transmitter on board the *Mi Amigo* in 1965.

Founder of Radio Caroline, Ronan O'Rahilly, on the tender heading back to Harwich after a visit to the *Mi Amigo*. The young Irishman started the station when he was 23 years old, changing the face of broadcast music in Britain.

Around Harwich and *Dovercourt*

A branch line train hauled by an N2 locomotive passes youngsters in the Hangings
as it approaches Dovercourt Bay station during the winter of 1955.

Harwich Quay in 1960 before the sea wall was rebuilt with cars lining the quay, the Angel pub in the background.

A similar photograph of the quay taken further along. The old GER Hotel is in the background.

Cars lining the quay before the sea wall was rebuilt and raised in about 1960.

Subsidence on the quay between the Ha'Penny Pier and ship yard, c. 1960s.

An aerial view of Harwich looking up Eastgate Street with the house on the corner of Castlegate Street and the Alma pub on the right, c. 1960s.

West Street in the 1950s
before demolition started.

Demolition by
Callaghan's starts
in West Street in
the 1950s.

An early view of Church Street, Harwich with St Nicholas Church towering above the street scene.
The sign for the Hanover dining room is hanging over the right-hand side of the street at the bottom.
Harwich Radio and Cycle Supplies are front, right.

Demolition at Harwich in readiness for redevelopment, c. 1950s.

Kings Head Street dereliction, c. 1950s.

David Wills' 'Gold Medal Baker' shop in Church Street. The Regal cinema poster is advertising films from 1959 ('Sleeping Beauty') and 1960 ('Cone of Silence').

Looking through St Austins Lane some time in the 1960s. These buildings were demolished for new flats.

The corner of the Half Moon in St Austins Lane looking through to Kings Head Street, c. 1960s.

Church Street in 1970.

West Street before restoration in the 1960s.

Kings Quay Street
before demolition
in the 1950s.

Church Street, looking towards the sea in June 1970.

St Austins Lane looking towards Kings Quay Street with the Half Moon,
then an antiques shop, on the left, in June 1970.

The corner of St
Austins Lane and
Kings Quay Street,
c. 1960s. The
building nearest the
camera became
a restaurant.

A 1950s view by the High Lighthouse showing the West Street service garage, later to become the Anglia Fruit Farms warehouse and workshop.

The Harbour office (left) in Kings Quay Street in April 1967.

Church Street in the winter of 1957-8, with the snow-capped roof of the Co-op owned pub, the Wheatsheaf, on the left.

'The Plain' or Kings Quay Street in the winter of 1957-8 looking towards the Globe and F&C Nichols' general store with Middleton's shop on the left.

Bathside Garage in 1963.

A thatcher restoring the roof of a building in Cliff Park, c. 1960s.

The Redoubt in 1968 before the Harwich Society took it under their wing and restored it.

Formerly used in the ship yard, the Harwich treadwheel crane photographed in the 1970s is the only one of its type which survives today in Britain. It was moved to its present home on St Helen's Green in about 1932.

Beacon Hill Fort, November 1974. Built originally to defend the Port of Harwich and disarmed after the First World War, it was bought back into service in 1940. It was decommissioned in 1956.

Built in 1911, the Electric Palace is one of the oldest purpose-built cinemas to survive in this country complete with its silent screen, original projection room and ornamental frontage still intact. This photograph was taken in April 1974, before the Electric Palace Trust was formed to restore the cinema to its former glory.

A flooded Bathside Infants School, c. 1968.

The collapse of the promenade along Marine Parade near Cliff Park in December 1967.

Tumilty's electrical shop in Dovercourt, c. 1960s. In the basement they sold all the latest records.

Miss Gage's confectionery shop stood opposite Cliff Park on the corner of Waddesdon Road.
At the rear was Mr Green's Fish and Chip shop, a popular haunt for youngsters calling in for a
three-penny bag of chips after swimming. The waste ground is now shops and the job centre;
the next building is the outer wall of Tumilty's shop, c. 1960s.

Denney's fishmongers in Dovercourt High Street, c. 1960s.

The junction of Bay Road and the High Street looking along Station Road towards Dovercourt railway station.
On the left is Beales Amusement Arcade, c. 1960s.

Orwell Terrace, c. 1960s. This was part of John Bagshaw's design in the 1850s for 'Dovercourt New Town' planned to rival Brighton. His projects were never to come to fruition after he became bankrupt in 1859.

The striking building of Lloyds Bank, Dovercourt High Street in 1964.

Coopers the stationers was opposite Sewell's in the High Street, 1964.

Dovercourt High Street. The Eastern National bus is heading for Low Road past Woolworth's and Fred Rose's Estate Agents. There were no yellow lines then, c. 1960s.

A 1960s view of the High Street looking towards the traffic lights.

The High Street in 1956 looking past Basham's barber shop on the corner of Orwell Terrace
with the King's Arms opposite.

Mrs Sewell's grocer's shop in the High Street, in 1964, well known for its fine produce.
At that time Dovercourt had seven grocery shops.

The Empire Cinema in Kingsway boarded up. Built in 1913 to seat 500 people, the cinema closed in 1938 when the Regal opened. It was demolished in 1963. The photograph is presumably from 1957, the year when the Regent's film, 'The Unholy Wife', starring Diana Dors, was released. The Regal was showing 'The Steel Bayonet', a British war film in which the young Michael Caine had a small role, also released in 1957.

Victoria Street flooded after heavy rain in August 1968.

Repairs to the sea wall near the lighthouses on Dovercourt beach in 1965.

Demolition of the brick beach huts on Dovercourt promenade, April 1969.

A lonely soul watches the snow plough clearing the High Street in the winter of 1957-8 at the junction with Kingsway. Smith's the greengrocer's stands opposite. The machine is a Chaseside 'Hi-Lift' Shovel fitted with a bulldozer attachment and it is based on a Fordson E27N Major tractor.

The match must go on – snow did not stop matches in those days.
The Royal Oak ground in the winter of 1957-8, Len Clover wielding the shovel.

Upper Dovercourt looking down Main road at the junction with Clarkes Road to the left. c. 1960s. Sutherland's the chemist is at the junction; Honey's shop advertises Daniell's Ales next to the forecourt of the White Horse.

A picket line for the seaman's strike in July 1972 on the Parkeston Road leading to Parkeston Quay.

People and *Events*

Life-Boat day, August 1976, with the 'Bernard's Girls' aboard *Margaret Graham*.
Girls from the Bernard's factory would dress up every year to raise money for the RNLI.

One of the local pub teams taking part in the whaler race as part of the Water Carnival in June 1970.

Morris Men performing outside the Angel in July 1970.

Harwich County High School's performance of *Iolanthe* in March 1978.

Harwich County High School's performance of Gilbert & Sullivan's *The Gondoliers* in July 1973.

Broadcaster Alan Freeman performing at the Trades Fair held at the old Yeast Factory, September 1968.

A Trinity House signwriter concentrates on his work, c. 1960s.

Jiving to one of the groups which performed at the regular Saturday night dances at the Cliff Pavilion in the 1960s. Groups such as The Martells, Jimmy Pilgrim and the Strangers, Dekka and the Diamonds, Zodiacs and Evergreens were regular groups at these dances.

The old ticket office at the ship yard with youngsters jumping into the 'oggin, c. 1950s.

Young army cadets on parade at their headquarters in Barrack Lane, c. 1960s.

A once regular sight – the army preparing to board ship at Navyard prior to going on exercise in June 1969.

1960s youngsters eagerly waiting for the kitchels to be thrown from the balcony of the Town Hall by the new Mayor during the annual Mayor Making Day. Kitchels are spicy buns made to a secret recipe.

Waiting for the kitchels in 1960.

Mr Ethelbert Good, part of the Harwich Good / Britton fishing family, on Ha'Penny Pier in his latter years, c. 1960s.

Fred Good, a well-known
Harwich fisherman and
councillor, tending his nets
on Ha'Penny Pier in 1963.

Tom Thomas and
Vic Good sifting
shrimps, c. 1960s.

The postman calls, the lady of the house comes to the door to collect her mail, c. 1950s.

Milkman Arnold Osborne from Vicarage Farm Dairy hands a young customer his daily 'pinta', c. 1960s.

Brownies in the back garden of the Vicarage in 1964 when the Reverend Johnson was Vicar.
The brownies are Sarah Ibbotson, Susan Lambert and Barbara Allen.

Pickets in Valley Road when the caravan factory was on strike, c. 1965.

A trade union parade through Dovercourt High Street in 1965.

In the cold winter of 1963-4, youngsters in the Hangings were taking their sledges to the Toboggan Field at the rear of Shaftesbury Avenue. Every evening after school and at weekends until dark hundreds of children, their parents and sledges would speed down the steep slope and through the gap in the bramble bush at the bottom. The field is now The Vines housing estate.

Remembrance Day in the 1950s at Minesweepers Memorial with local dignitaries and army officers probably from the Transit Camp.

On Saturday 1 June 1966 the new Fire Station was opened in Fronks Road. The retained firemen are being inspected in the Drill Yard by Alderman GE Rose, Chairman of the Fire Brigade Committee. With him are (helmeted) Station Officer Jim Howard; hidden by the helmet, Mr LE Hostler, Mayor of Harwich, and Chief Fire Officer Ellis. Firemen on parade: Bill Newman, Ken Goldsmith, Cliff Reeves, Don Wrycraft, Tony Parr, Tom Billings, David Newman and Sub-Officer Harry Smith. Just out of picture is Leading Fireman Jim Upson.

Presentation of Trophies for Harwich winning the Brigade Efficiency Competition in 1964 outside the old Fire Station in Harwich. (Left to right): Don Martin, Mike Barrago, Deputy Chief Barnard, Mick Heggarty, Divisional Officer Cashman, Eric Tyrell, D Cook. Officer in charge Jim Howard was off duty.

Fireman Mike Barrago peers inside the bonnet of a burnt-out car after the the fire
which destroyed Smith's Motors in July 1973.

Burnt-out beach huts at Dovercourt West End in 1964.

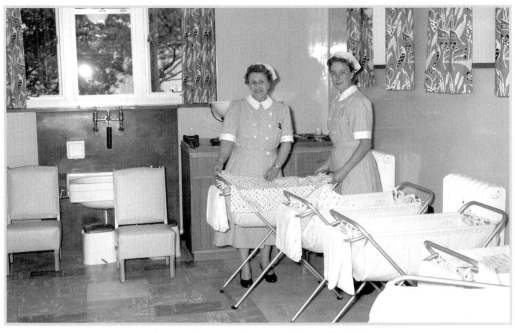

Nurses in the maternity unit at Dovercourt's Fryatt Hospital, c. 1960s.

Girls at work on Fine Fare labels in the overprinting section of Tickopres, the Dovercourt printers, c. 1960s.

Bernard's factory was well known for producing uniforms for the Navy and all the F

rd's had sales offices at naval ports and Gibraltar in their heyday, c. late 1950s.

Girls busy sewing uniforms on Singer sewing machines at Bernard's, c. late 1950s.

Bernard's girls in a festive mood.

The start of the Soapbox Derby on Marine Parade by the Minesweepers Memorial, in about 1960.
The course ran down Donkey Hill to the promenade.

A helicopter display at the summer carnival on the Barrack Field, c. 1960.
The Air Sea Rescue helicopter lifted a pillion passenger from the despatch rider's motorcycle.

The summer Carnival Parade passes through Dovercourt High Street in 1960.

The summer Carnival Parade travelling down Donkey Hill to the promenade, 1960 (top picture)
and reaching the Phoenix Hotel, sadly now demolished (bottom).

The Queen and Prince Philip meeting local dignitaries outside the town hall before boarding the Royal Yacht *Britannia* at Parkeston Quay in 1958.

Schoolchildren line the route outside Main Road County Primary School, now demolished, waiting to see the Queen in 1958.

Well-wishers of all ages seek vantage points while waiting to see Her Majesty in 1958.

In May 1981 her Majesty the Queen paid another visit.

Competitors at the Parkeston Shrove Tuesday pancake race in March 1973.

Switchboard operators at Dovercourt's telephone exchange, c. 1960s.

A float at the Guy Carnival in 1982. The carnival has been a much-loved Harwich tradition, going for over 150 years. The carnival was started by ship yard workers to 'guy' (take the mickey out of) their employers and has nothing to do with Guy Fawkes night.

Revellers enjoying the Guy Carnival in November 1968.

Fancy dress at the Guy Carnival, November 1969 (top) and the late 1950s (bottom).

Fancy dress on a Guy Carnival float, c. 1960s.

Summer Carnival Queen's parade aboard the MV *Brightlingsea*, c. 1960.

SPORTS

The 1965 Festival of Sport at the Sir Anthony Deane School, with the Harwich Motor Cycle Club showing their
skills with a motoball team. Bob Ramplin and John Mowle are going for goal against 'keeper John Culley.
Mick Hales and Malcolm Pilbro are in the background.

Sports Day at the Sir Anthony Deane School in 1964.

Pupils cheer on their favourites at the Sir Anthony Deane School Sports Day in 1964.

Mayflower County Primary School netball team 1959, winners of a local tournament. Included are Carolyn Bergen, Barbara Chittock, Carol Calver, Jennifer Brown, Kathleen Moonlight, Mrs Valerie Tibbenham, Chris Bentley and Jenny Chapman.

The newly formed Harwich and Dovercourt rugby club at the Sir Anthony Deane School pitch before the move to the new Low Road clubhouse, c. 1963.

Harwich County High School girls' hockey team c. 1965-6 with Miss Hawkins and headmaster Mr Welburn.

Harwich High School football team with Mr Welburn and Mr Hall the sports master, c. 1965-6.

Harwich County High School girls' tennis team with headmaster Mr Welburn, c. 1965-6.

Harwich County High School cricket team with Mr Welburn and Mr Hall, c. 1965-6.

Harwich Junior League representative team which played Clacton Junior League on the Royal Oak, Easter Monday 1961.

The Dovercourt
roller hockey team
in the 1950s.

The 'Shrimpers' manager Eric Armstrong discusses tactics in October 1972 with Steve Devaux, Derek Edwards, Alan Fletcher, Mick Clarke, Barry Vernon, Tony Armstrong and Don James.

Harwich and Parkeston football club in the 1960s (back row): Howard Moxon, Steve Page, John Yellop, Ron Mitchell, Roger Page, Steve Szemerenyi. (Front row): Gordon Claydon, Howard Osborne, Steve Devaux, Phil Palmer, Mike Nicholl.

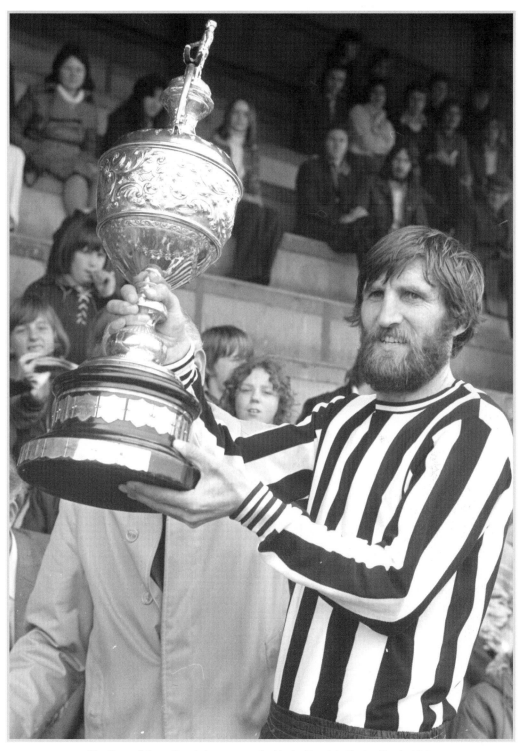

The 'Legend' Steve Page being presented with the Harwich Charity Cup in 1973.

St Joseph's school football team with their trophies, c. 1960s.

Two school teams, competitors in the Fisherman's Cup Final, c. 1960s. The Fisherman's Cup was donated by Harwich fishermen to be played for by local primary schools.

School football team on the Barrack Field, c. 1960s.

A school football team on the Barrack Field, c. 1960s.

School football team on the Barrack Field with referee Brian Button, c. 1960s

Ramsey United FC winners of the 'Strover Cup' in about 1958, a youth football under-17 competition named after the Rev. Strover. The players are Peter Green, Michael Day, Adrian Heard, Tony 'Lofty' Clifford, Bernie Sadler (holding the cup), Tony Carter, Mick 'Nog' Jennings, Paul Bradford, Terry Howlett, Malcolm Musgrove and John Baldry.

Other Photograph Books from Old Pond Publishing

Acknowledgements

ALF SMITH

Freelance photographer Alfred Smith worked for many years from Shaftesbury Avenue, Dovercourt. He became an acknowledged specialist in marine photography, his work being used in technical reports, books and shipping line brochures.

'Smithy' was born a Yorkshireman in Morley. During the Second World War he served in North Africa with the 48th Royal Tank Regiment, and he later worked as a demolition specialist with the Control Commission in Germany. In 1952 he and his wife Ada 'Topsy' came to Dovercourt and established their successful photography business.

An active member of the Harwich branch of the RNLI, Alfred Smith died in February 1994 aged 71.

Alfred Smith's negatives were the source of this compilation by David Kindred and Peter Goodwin. The negatives were placed in the hands of the Harwich Society and after being stored in various places since Alfred's death were handed to David Kindred in 2009 for digitising and preservation.

However, when David looked for Alf's negative file books which would have recorded details about the photographs, including the date they were taken, he found that only a few had survived. When an accurate date is known it is included in the caption. Otherwise, historical events help to date many of the photographs. Where no date is known, an approximate date is given, guided by the negative number.

This has been done to help place the photographs in the correct era. The authors apologise for any inaccuracies.

This book has been made possible through the kind help of Dave Whittle of the Harwich Society, Ken Brand, Trinity House, Tony Carter, Jim Howard, Keith Lawrence, Geoffrey Britton, Dave Lubbock, John Steer and Stuart Gibbard.

THE AUTHORS

The captions for the book have been researched and written by Peter Goodwin, born and bred in Dovercourt, and the author of *Harwich & Dovercourt Pubs*. Apart from being a keen collector of local photographs and local history, Peter is a founder member and President of Harwich Motorcycle Club and a supporter for sixty years of Harwich & Parkeston FC. Peter also takes a keen interest in Thames sailing barges and steam locomotives. The book is dedicated to the memory of his good friend John Mowle who sadly passed away in August 2009. John was the author of two local books, *Harwich & Dovercourt volumes 1 and 2*.

David Kindred was for over forty years a member of the photographic team at the *East Anglian Daily Times*, based at the newspaper's head office in Ipswich. He left full-time employment with the company in 2004 as picture editor to the *Evening Star* and since has pursued an interest in researching vintage photographs. David has been the author of several books of vintage photographs of Suffolk. This is his first featuring Essex. David took on the task of looking through many thousands of negatives mostly taken on 120 roll film and rolled tight with an elastic band round them, many of which had perished over more than forty years.